The
S🔒crets
to Getting
A's in College

7

Cover design and interior layout by Christine Howard.
Illustrations by Anderson Carman.
Editing by Emme Raus.

Printed in the United States of America

First Printing, 2017

ISBN 978-0-9984122-0-7

To my wife who supported me through my MBA, endless hours of work, and my life. You are the best mother and partner I know. I am blessed to have you in my life.

Contents

Foreword

This field guide is designed to be concise and to deliver proven tips, tools, and habits needed to achieve the highest grades possible at college. By using the seven secrets you will increase comprehension, recollection, and understanding of the materials you study regardless of the topic. Most importantly, you will *learn how to learn* – a skill you can use for a lifetime.

So, dive in. Keep it handy as a reference. Reread it periodically to pick up additional ideas and remind yourself of the practices described.

Why Try To Get A's?

While A's themselves are a good accomplishment, this book is about more than just getting good grades. If all you want is the diploma, then you can get A's (and B's and C's) several ways including: cramming for tests the night before, having other people do your homework, and even cheating on tests.

So, why strive for A's? Class ranking, pride, bragging rights and more quickly come to mind. In most cases, it is true that a higher Grade Point Average (GPA) will also help you land your first or even second job. According to Tracy Brisson and confessionsofateacherrecruiter.com, "If your GPA is under 3.0 and you're just graduating, you're going to struggle and you need to be prepared for that."[1] It is also true that employers and graduate schools look at your GPA as one of many measures of what you know. But a GPA also reveals much more about you than what you have learned.

[1] The Blog. The Opportunities Project, 2 May 2014. Web. 3 Jan. 2016. <www.confessionso-fateacherrecruiter.com/blog/ 2014/05/02/sorry-recent-graduate-your-gpa-will-impact-your-job-search>.

If you read this book and do nothing, try nothing, or change nothing in how you approach college - it is wasted time. Stop reading now. I challenge you to take action and try these seven tips. Much like telling people your New Year's resolution, sharing your goals will help you stay on track. Enlist the help and support of friends by posting your commitment to do these things on social media platforms like Facebook, Twitter, Instagram, Pinterest, Snapchat, etc. so it is not easy to forget or dismiss. Provide updates periodically on your achievements or challenges and even your failures to gain additional support and encouragement too.

A high GPA can be a key indicator of the "never give up" attitude known as personal tenacity. It can also be a sign of personal discipline, overall character and ability to work with others. Degree programs focus on specific majors such as engineering, computer science, history, fine arts, biology and more. However, successful completion of a wide range of core courses ranging from mathematics, writing, sciences, arts, natural sciences, history and others are more often than not required to graduate.

It is easier to perform well in a subject you enjoy and are interested in learning about. Earning A's in courses you care less about (or not at all) takes more effort, open mindedness, and discipline. These are traits that will serve you well in business and life.

The measure of true success comes from doing what you love, and achieving your goals – whatever those goals may be. The more you love what you do, the more successful you will be; whether your goal is to run corporations, cure cancer, achieve social justice, run a small bookstore, live a religious life, teach underprivileged children or anything else. If you really want to be good at what you do, you must become a person who loves to learn.

2500 years ago, the Greek philosopher Heraclitus declared, "The only constant in life is change".[2] There are examples of change all around us today that support his claim. One example is the adoption of mobile phone usage. Apple introduced the iPhone in 2007. The iPhone made instant information accessible to anyone, anywhere as the most affordable and user-friendly smartphone ever. As a result, mobile phone ownership skyrocketed with the total number growing more than six times from 172 million in 2009 to 1.4 billion in 2015.[3] Also, in 2015, the number of U.S. households with cellphone-only communications surpassed households with working land-line telephones for this first time in history.[4] South Korea's mobile phone penetration rate topped 100% in 2010, meaning that there are more mobile phones in use in the country than there are people.[5]

What will the next 10, 20 or 50 years bring? Although you will learn many specific things in college – what you are really doing is forming habits that teach you how to learn throughout your life. The struggle to achieve A's is a foundation for lifelong success. While achieving an A in a course is great today, it is a temporary measure of your success. Learning how to learn by striving for A's in college generates a lifetime of opportunity to grow, succeed, and accomplish great things – whatever YOU define as success throughout your lifetime.

[2] Wikipedia. 18 Nov. 2015. Web. 27 Dec. 2015. <https://en.wikipedia.org/wiki/Hera-clitus>.
[3] https://www.statista.com/statistics/263437/global-smartphone-sales-to-end-users-since-2007/
[4] www.statista.com/chart/2072/landline-phones-in-the-united-states
[5] Korea's Smartphone Population Tops Milestone. The Wall Street Journal, 28 July 2014. Web. 2 Dec. 2015.

The Four Letter Word

Getting A's is more about discipline than being inherently smart. Yes, a few very smart people are gifted to the point where they just naturally understand the material. More than likely though, if you get to know these people instead of admiring or fearing them from a distance, you'd see that 9 out of 10 of them have to work hard to earn what they get.

Life is a series of circumstances, chance, and choices. The choices you make are the only thing you can really control. Many people are born into certain circumstances and even the best statisticians can't control chance (sometimes known as luck). At college, you make many choices for the first time in your life. Balancing work and relaxation is a major challenge, one that every student deals with.

Choosing how you spend your time is a natural struggle as you evolve from a highly-dependent person within a family setting to an independent, capable, and self-sustaining adult in a world where you make every decision. Like every choice in life, you can expect to make some mistakes – and learn from them too. Making good choices comes down to three things.

1. **Maintaining focus and a clear goal.**
   Examples: Earn a degree, stay healthy, make friends, get enough rest, experience relationships, earn a living, be worthy of love, help others and more.

2. **Taking advantage of the opportunities presented.**
   Examples: Being accepted to one or more colleges, choosing which people or groups to spend time with, the freedom to eat anything you want in the cafeteria, staying up all night playing video games and more.

3. **Discipline to do what it takes to achieve your goals.**
   Examples: Don't skip classes, actively participate in class, avoid too much partying, don't have unprotected sex to safeguard your health, limit time playing video games to avoid becoming an addict that cannot disconnect or manage relationships in the physical world and more.

This leads to the four-letter word everybody loves to hate: **WORK**. To get A's, you are going to have to work for it. Work is not a bad thing – especially if you love what you do or love the results of your hard work. Everyone wants to relax and have fun, but if all we do is relax we will become lazy, bored, and unfulfilled. In other words, without work there would be no joy in relaxing.

Work gets a bad rap when you don't enjoy what you do to earn a living. A big part of college is taking a wide variety of classes. It is common to wonder why you are required to take certain classes, especially if they don't appear to be directly related to your major. For example, what does mathematics have to do with a degree in art history, or how does philosophy relate to a degree in mechanical engineering?

Deep down, everything is related and even if you never use what you learned in those courses again, you may have learned that you chose the right major and do not want to focus on other areas of study. However, you may also find a new subject that sparks your interest into learning more and broadening your base of knowledge and interests.

Don't let the idea and reality of needing to work hard discourage, frighten, or annoy you. Work may be a four-letter word, but unlike vulgar four-letter words, it can lead to a life of comfort, well-being, and security.

The Seven Secrets

While the seven secrets may seem simple and obvious, the difference between wanting something and achieving it is to actually take action; try it, adjust and improve on your last attempt; fail, try again, and succeed. As mentioned in chapter two, discipline is a critical element of success. It is not easy, but remember this: if it was easy, anyone could do it. Just by reading this book, you have chosen to invest your time. By taking action on these ideas, you are already in the top 25% of people who will read this book. Enough said, lets jump in!

Secret #1:

Go to every class.

This is your Number 1 priority. Period. No excuses. Just do it every day.

It seems simple enough and I'm sure you have every intention of doing it, but it comes back to being on your own for the first time, your level of personal discipline, and making good decisions. At college no one is going to check on you. No one is going to remind you, and no one is going to care if you actually go to class. Your roommate, your Resident Advisor (RA) and your professors will go about their business without ever giving you a thought. It is very easy to roll over in bed when the alarm rings, or stay in a warm bed when it is cold and snowy outside. In fact, college is the perfect environment to skip classes in and tell yourself, "It's only one class, I can make it up later."

Going to class means more than just physically being there too. You will notice several students in class sleeping, texting, surfing Facebook or Instagram, and more. These people will get no benefit from being in class. Going to every class means you need to:

1. **Be on-time or 5-10 minutes early.**

2. **Find a good seat (see rule number six).**

3. **Have your questions ready.**

4. **Be alert and eager to listen and learn.**

By doing these four things you will be in top form to absorb the material. In fact, you can significantly reduce studying time for tests because you will be more likely to understand and recall the material quickly and clearly.

Would you buy a seat at a rock concert or NFL game and then send someone else to record it for you? Of course not! But this is the same idea as skipping a class and then asking someone to record it for you. Your professors are not rock stars and in many cases may be boring (to you), and possibly even egotistical and rude. But, you still need to attend every class!

Let's assume you are paying $10,000 per semester. With a course load of 15 hours per semester, you are paying an average of $44 per hour for lectures.[6] If your school costs $15,000 or $20,000 a semester, the cost per class jumps to $66 or $88 per hour or more! Missing 2-3 classes in one semester can add up to a ticket to a major event! So don't miss out. Be there yourself (in every class) to interpret the material, learn it, and decide for yourself how to use that knowledge.

Finally, go to bed at a reasonable time. Usually, this is before 11p.m. or midnight when you have class the next morning. Yes, you are independent now (woohoo!), and a big part of staying independent at school, work, and in life is to know how much sleep you need to function at 100% – and then choosing to go to sleep so you get the rest you need. Your mom is not there to remind you or tuck you in. So again, it is up to you now.

---

[6] Fifteen credit hours per week=15 hours in class per week. There are 15 weeks per semester for a total of 225 lecture hours per semester. $10,000/225=$44/per class.

Secret #2:

Do the homework... on time.

OK, back to the four letter word: WORK.

College classes move fast. Staying up to date and not falling behind are critical to keeping pace, learning and succeeding in college. You can expect to cover up to twice as much material per year compared to high school. For example, expect to cover the same amount of material you learned during a one-year high-school course in only one semester of college. Many times, tomorrow's lesson depends on you understanding today's material. At this pace, it is necessary to review and practice the material taught in each class, and to reinforce it in your mind in order to prepare for the next class.

Don't panic though; millions of people do this successfully every year and with the right approach, so can you. Everyone is different, so besides the commitment and discipline to do the homework on time, you may need to try different methods of studying to determine how you learn best. Some people are early risers and think most clearly in the morning, while others are night owls who like to take naps in the afternoon and thrive on the peace and quiet of late-night studying. Some people study best in the library while others hate the library and study best in their dorm room or with friends. Whatever your style, the key to success is finishing assignments on time and with complete, well-thought-out answers.

Show you are serious about learning by asking the teacher specific questions about the homework assignment in the next class (see secret #3). Many teachers will assign seemingly ridiculous amounts of homework. The class is used to give you an overview of the material while the homework is how you learn more about the material in depth, and sometimes major amounts of homework are actually needed to learn the material. Sometimes, huge amounts of homework are assigned to test how serious or committed to the subject or degree you really are. This "weeding out" technique is used to produce high-quality graduates. Those who are uninterested, unwilling or unable to complete the homework will change majors or even drop out of college all together.

Secret #3:

Make sure the teacher knows who you are.

There are different ways to make sure the teacher knows who you are and the techniques to use can vary from teacher to teacher depending on their personality, ego, and how open-minded they are. The key to success is to show a genuine interest in the subject.

Show interest in the subject by asking a few questions during the semester. Try not to overdo it here. You do not have to be the teacher's pet. It's also important to make a positive impression so be inquisitive but not overbearing or obnoxious. It's good to ask for clarification anytime, especially on complex topics and new concepts. Also remember to be respectful. You will not gain anything by trying to outsmart a teacher or trying to prove them wrong.

If the teacher is open-minded and encourages active participation, you might consider challenging a statement or theory that is being taught, but always in a respectful manner. Learning comes from testing ideas and debating different viewpoints. Most truly great accomplishments and advancements occurred because someone refused to believe a widely-accepted limitation or the status quo. Equally true is that nothing truly great ever happened by blindly accepting everything one is told.

It's also important to go to each teacher's office outside of classroom hours. Doing this at least once during the semester takes effort and gets noticed. Use the time to ask questions about recent lectures and ask specific questions about homework assignments. While you are there, ask if there are any ways to earn some extra credit – especially if you fumbled over a test or quiz and now need to recover BIG TIME in order to get that A. Extra credit is rare but it never hurts to ask.

Note: Make sure the actual teacher knows who you are. Having a Teacher's Assistant (or "TA") who knows you can also be helpful, but not as important in the end – unless the TA is actually grading the work, and really running the class.

Another important benefit of having the teacher know who you are is the chance for them to recommend you for internships and special projects. These can be paid or unpaid opportunities – and they can't recommend you if they don't know who you are. Internships and special projects are the early steps of professional networking, and networking is a skill you will need throughout your career to remain relevant in your chosen industry and to locate good jobs.

Secret #4:

A few days before a test ... study a little!

Review and rewrite your class notes. A good practice is to review and then condense and summarize your notes onto a few "study sheets." By doing this, you are reinforcing the material in your memory and at the same time, reliving it. Rewriting and summarizing notes requires concentration, and concentration helps your brain recall facts, complex theories, and details needed on exams.

The more senses you use when studying material, the better you will learn it. For example, reading your notes takes only eye sight, while rewriting your notes takes eyesight and the tactile sense to feel the pencil in your hand. If you actually say the words out loud while you are writing them, it's even better. Notice that I am talking about actually writing your notes on paper. While typing into a computer can be OK, it's too easy to copy/paste notes from a website or other online resources, and you lose the tactile benefit of actually writing it out longhand. Use the four helpful tips below when preparing for exams to achieve the best possible score.

1. Do some practice problems. For classes like mathematics and science, there are always extra problems in the back of each chapter. Often the answers to several problems are provided so you can even check your answers. It is common to have problems on exams that are similar to those in the text book. The values, names, and descriptions may be different, but they are the same basic problems. So if you learn them from the book ahead of time, it can really pay off on the exams. Additional practice problems are often available online too. Many people have already taken these classes, so much of the material you will be learning is out there if you look for it.

2. Working on practice problems with a group.
Working on these practice problems in a study group is another great way to learn and reinforce what you know. If you can explain how to solve a problem to a teammate, you can be assured that you really understand the material. If you are not sure how to approach or solve a problem, someone in your study group may be able to help you. If no one on the team knows how to do it, then working together and collaborating on the solution can really help too (see secret #5 below for additional ideas).

3. Prepare in advance, a little at a time. What if the first time you drove a car was the day before your driver's license test? Ridiculous, right? The same idea applies to college exams. Waiting until the night before and then cramming for an exam is a sure way to lower your grade. It may be possible, and even necessary to do this a few times in your college career, but as a practice, it just doesn't work. Much in the same way that sports teams practice every day and especially before a game, you also need to practice ahead of time to succeed on your exams.

4. Talk to the teacher ahead of time in class or during office hours. Ask what specific topics will be on the test/exam and make sure you are familiar and competent in those sections. If you are confused on a topic, ask for help! ASK for a study guide or some additional problems. ASK for some extra help. ASK for websites and anything else they can provide. By asking, they will know you care about their topic and this in itself is a very good thing (see secret #3 for additional thoughts).

Secret #5:

Form a study group.

Be selective: form groups ONLY with people that also want to get A's. Avoid people who are too socially oriented, party (too much), take drugs, skip class, etc. Note: It may not always be easy to tell these groups apart when you first meet, Beware of and kick out slackers, bottom feeders, and goof-offs; even if they're your friends. Remember that you get to choose who you study with so make good choices!

It is always helpful to discuss things with others. You get different viewpoints, learn things you didn't know (or maybe just didn't understand), and you get to reinforce what you do know already. When possible, hold study groups in a room where there is a white board so you can capture ideas and draw diagrams. Keep discussions on track by creating a separate list of unrelated questions called a parking lot to capture tangential topics and illustrate ideas.[7]

When possible, take turns going up to the board and solving problems. If stuck, ask the group how they might approach the problem. Figure it out together and make sure you understand what is going on. Sometimes none of you will know what to do, so look online for hints and if that still doesn't help, write the question down and visit the teacher during office hours as a group. This will show the teacher that you are all committed to understanding the subject (see secret #3).

---

[7] Meeting Tangents Suck! Try the Parking Lot. Perf. Jon Petz. YouTube. BoringMeetings-Suck, 7 Sept. 2007. Web. 15 Nov. 2015.

Sometimes, a TA or teacher will schedule structured review sessions before an exam. Always attend every one of these sessions because it is extra help presented on a silver platter! Sometimes the TA has seen the exam and they know the material very well, so listen to what they have to say at these sessions. Usually, they will take attendance and again, your participation helps to demonstrate you care enough to put in the extra effort needed to do well.

Secret #6:

Always sit up front.

This is especially true when you are in a class with a large number of students. Some lecture halls can hold 300-400 people and when you sit in the back, it is very easy to get distracted by people who are checking their email, surfing the web, sleeping, etc. When you sit in the first three-to-five rows, it feels like you are in a class of 30-40 instead of 300-400.

You are there to learn something and the front of the room is where the action is. Whether you are in row three or row thirty-five, it doesn't matter what is going on behind you. Also, once class starts, anyone who is late never enters through the front doors. Instead they enter through doors in the rear. If you sit in the back of the room, every time a door opens and closes or someone's computer screen flashes, it breaks your concentration.

You may not even recognize these distractions until later when you missed some important comment by the teacher or a question that was asked by another student. By sitting up front, you will be part of the discussions, more engaged in the topic being taught, and far less vulnerable to interruptions caused by fellow students. As an added bonus, sitting up front will help the teacher recognize your face (supporting secret #3).

Secret #7:

Start each semester focused and running.

College is a new environment and it is easy to feel overwhelmed. If you started slowly or relaxed and expect to gain momentum during the semester, you are likely to fall behind and then struggle to keep up with the workload and demands of the curriculum. To succeed, you need to start in top form, with maximum energy and commitment, or "running into the semester." Start each semester RUNNING, with full energy and determination. College is challenging and by the end of each semester you will most likely be exhausted. If you start the semester with only average energy and discipline, you may run out of steam shortly after mid-term exams, resulting in poor academic performance overall.

If you think of each semester as a marathon race then you will understand the need to start and end strong. If you are tired, lazy, and struggling up front it will be nearly impossible to recover and achieve good grades, much less A's. Your level of energy will naturally decline during the semester because of the workload and sustained effort required to complete each course.

The amount of work and determination required to complete some semesters may be so intense that if you "run" into the semester you will be "crawling" out after final exams. The good news is that each semester has a defined finish line, so even if you are struggling and your level of energy is declining; remember that it is only fifteen weeks long. You can do anything for fifteen weeks!

Final Thoughts

As you think about the seven secrets, keep in mind that these are the foundation for college success and not the only ways to gain an advantage. Don't be fooled if they seem familiar or simple. In fact, most people may already know these, but most people do not get A's because they don't have a plan or they don't take the time to actually do these things.

You don't need to be a neuroscientist to understand that we all have conscious and unconscious thoughts. When you get stuck on a problem or subject and just "don't get it," give your subconscious brain a chance to process it for a while. If you let your brain rest, or actively use a different part of your brain, you may find that a new idea, the next step, and sometimes the answer to the problem comes to you.

A good way to activate the subconscious brain is to do something completely different. According to Michael Michalko, creativity expert and author of Thinkertoys, "a majority of scientists, artists, and writers report that they get their best ideas and insights when not thinking about the problem."[8] Take a walk, jog, or a quick nap. Read a magazine on a completely different topic. Watch a silly movie that doesn't take concentration or involve deep plots. Then look at the original problem and try again. If this doesn't work talk with your study group, visit the teacher's office outside of class, or review the study guide you created from your condensed notes to spark new ideas.

Teachers are paid to teach you. But, it is not their job to help you get an A. It is your job to earn the A. Don't expect teachers to give out A's easily. Expect every teacher to make you work HARD for it. Then, the 2% of the time that you do happen to get an easier teacher, it's a bonus. If you really use the seven secrets, you'll already be ahead of the game and most of your classmates.

Striving for A's but not achieving an A is OK too. If you truly put full effort into a class and earn a B or C, be proud of that! Hard work and the strategies discussed in this guide will help you achieve the best possible grades that you can. It's also important to note that personal aptitude and other factors play a big part in the grades you will achieve. For example, some people are naturally more capable at learning math while struggling with languages and humanities.

---

[8] www.mindpowernews.com/CreativeThinkering.htm

The opposite can be true for people who have natural talents in the arts, but have a hard time with physics and the sciences. While few people will earn a 4.0 in college and every major has it's challenges, you can maximize your GPA - and more importantly learn about who you are and where you're interests and talents lie by using the seven secrets. Aligning your career with your interests is a recipe for lifelong success and personal fulfillment.

Finally, be sure to have fun at college too. Take time to goof-off! Make friends, relax, and even go wild sometimes. It is college after all and for most people, it is their first time having independence. Go to parties, participate in college activities and have fun. Just be safe – in every sense of the word – and make good decisions. More than anything in life, it is the decisions you make that define who you are.

Lessons learned from a B student

About the author

Bob Raus graduated with a 2.7 GPA for his undergraduate degree in Electrical Engineering. After working a few years he decided to enroll in an MBA degree program in order to advance his career. The company-sponsored graduate program required a grade of B or higher to be reimbursed for course fees which provided him the motivation to study and earn A's. He recognized patterns for success and formulated seven secrets to achieving A's during his graduate program. In the end, he achieved a 3.6 GPA for his MBA – a significant improvement and personal achievement.

Do you have comments, ideas or a story to share about how you achieved A's? Please submit them to www.facebook.com/7secretsforcollege or email secrettogettingas@gmail.com. Visit www.7secretsforcollege.com to learn more.

Notes

Notes

Notes

Notes

Notes

Notes